Introducing the one and only

# CICELY
## TYSON

written by
**Renée Watson**

illustrated by
**Sherry Shine**

**AMISTAD**
Books for Young Readers
*An Imprint of HarperCollins Publishers*

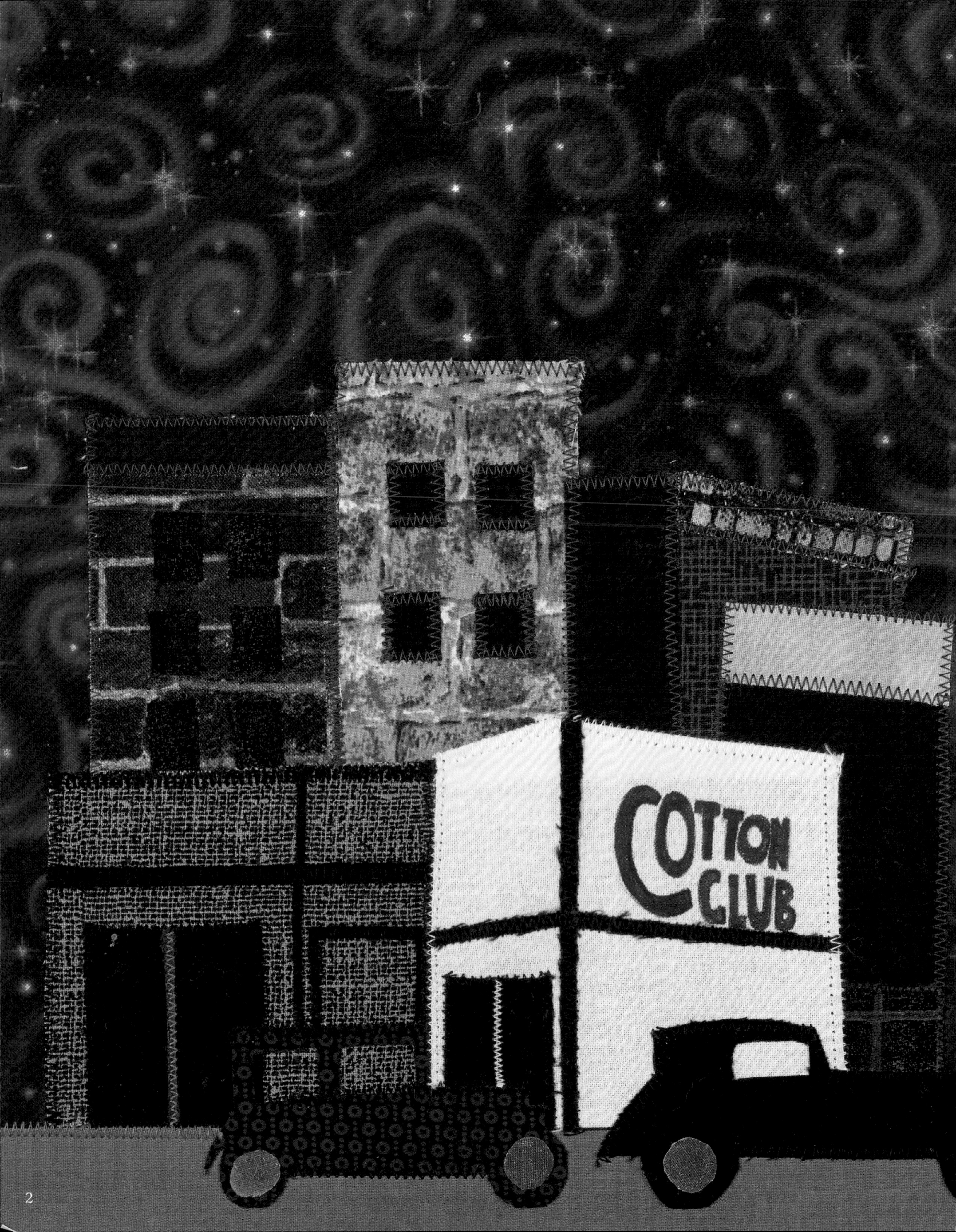
COTTON
CLUB

## 1920s

Black is Harlem.
Black is the buzz of a trumpet,
the soft brush tickling cymbal,
dark fingers tiptoeing on bass.

Black is the improv solo
going on and on.

Black endures.

W. 142 ST.
LENOX AVE.

# Cicely

Her father called her Heart String
because she was his first daughter, his beloved one.
Sometimes he called her String Bean
because she was thin and lanky.

Her mother called her Father Face
because her high cheekbones
made her look just like her daddy.

She was Lil Sis to her big brother, Melrose.
And Big Sister to baby Emily.

Cicely Tyson.

She was a bright light
shining in a world that was sometimes dark,
sometimes unjust.

Nine decades she lived:
96 years. 35,105 days.

With each sunrise she was determined
to be better than the day before, to do good in the world,
to shine her light brighter and brighter.

*This little light of mine,*
*I'm gonna let it shine.*
*Let it shine,*
*let it shine, let it shine!*

# December 19, 1924

She arrived to the world six days before Christmas.
Born in New York City, with roots stretching back to Nevis,
an island in the West Indies nestled between
the Atlantic Ocean and the Caribbean Sea.
The birthplace of her parents was never far
from her South Bronx home.
They brought the island with them.
Brought their patois, their love of green plantains
and fresh ginger. Brought their faith in God,
their prayers and hymns and dreams,
so many dreams they had for their baby girl.

# Prophecy

In the early hours of a June morning,
Cicely's mother took her out in the carriage
for a stroll around the neighborhood.
The Bronx was slowly waking up,
no car horns honking, no traffic jams,
just a gentle breeze from summer's sky,
soft like a kiss on the cheek.

A Jewish woman with tight brown curls
walked over to Cicely's mother
and looked in the carriage.

*Take care of that baby, the stranger said.*
*She's going to make you very proud one day.*

Cicely's momma held on to those words.
Tucked them in her heart for safekeeping.
Her baby girl was destined to impact the world.

## In the Beginning

Cicely loved sitting on her daddy's lap
while he strummed the guitar
and sang hymns.

As their father serenaded the family,
Melrose danced to the rhythm.
Cicely wiggled and moved her body, too,
listening to her daddy's soothing baritone voice.

The Tyson family didn't have a lot,
but they had each other.
And when the cares of the world
were too much to bear,
they turned to their faith to lift them up,
help them carry on.

*I'm gonna lay down my burdens
down by the riverside, down by the riverside,
down by the riverside . . . and study war no more.*

# An Ordinary Girl

A brown-skinned girl with twig legs
and not a whole lot of hair.

Cicely sucked her thumb from the day she was born,
so her teeth stuck out, and sometimes
kids at school teased her.

*Bucktoothed skinny girl!*
*Nappy head!*

She was even bullied for having
brown skin.

But her loved ones told her,
*Cicely, you are one of God's most gorgeous creations.*

At first Cicely didn't think their words were true,
but over time she believed them.

# Questions

Cicely's favorite word was *why*.
She believed it was the most important question.

Her mother grew weary with so many questions,
but Cicely was a curious girl:

*Why does the sun wake up on the east*
*and fall asleep on the west?*

*Why do clocks tick-tick-tick?*

*Why are some people sweet like honey,*
*and others just as mean as the sting of a bee?*

*Why are some people free*
*while others have never known freedom?*

*And why did that woman*
*with the thick curls say,*
*She's going to make you proud one day?*

*Why am I here,*
*on this earth,*
*at this moment?*

*Why?*

Soon, and very soon,
Cicely would have answers.

# Park Avenue, Between 111th & 116th

On Saturdays the family would go
to the West Indian outdoor market.
The women there dressed in colorful head wraps
and did more gossiping and laughing than shopping.

They swapped recipes
and fussed and bragged about their children.
Many of the women wondered
what Cicely would become.
She was so shy, surely she would not
grow up to do big, big things.

But Cicely knew she wasn't shy. She was quiet.
She liked watching and listening to the world around her.
She knew that one day she would surprise them all.

# How Do You Do?

Wearing a one-of-a-kind dress
made by her mother's hands,
Cicely sang her first solo at church.
A song to welcome the whole congregation.

*How do you do, my lovin' pastor, how do you do?*
*How do you do, choir, how do you do?*

Women with their wide, colorful Sunday hats
swayed and said, *Amen!*

Four deacons grabbed a wooden chair,
set Cicely on it, and lifted her up to the heavens,
carrying her around the sanctuary.

*How do you do, God's children, how do you do?*

Cicely felt something deep inside.
The light within her was burning
bright, bright, bright.

The audience didn't want her singing to end.
And neither did Cicely. She wanted to perform
again and again.

## 1930s–1950s

Black is turning nothing
into something,
turning something into
more than enough.

Black is a train ride up north,
saying goodbye to
the sweet fragrance of
magnolia trees,
the Whites Only segregation signs.
Black is knowing the beauty,
the brutality.

Black is the Tuskegee Airmen,
Adam Clayton Powell Jr.,
Jackie Robinson.

Black is Emmett Till
and Medgar Evers
and Rosa Parks
and that preacher man King.
Black is singing, always singing.
*We shall not, we shall not be moved.*

# Changes

Sometimes mommies and daddies don't get along.
Sometimes they argue and fight and lose the love
they had for each other.

Cicely was nine years old when her parents separated.
Even though they weren't in love anymore,
they loved Melrose, Cicely, and Emily,
and they vowed to always be there for their children.

Everything was changing
like the leaves on an autumn tree.

Her mother moved Melrose, Cicely, and Emily to a new home:
234 East 98th Street, at Third Avenue in East Harlem.
The apartment building's old stairs moaned and cried
as Cicely walked up the four flights. Cicely wanted to cry too.
She knew nothing would ever be the same.

But her mother assured her.
Even if her parents could not be with each other,
she was still loved, she was still loved.

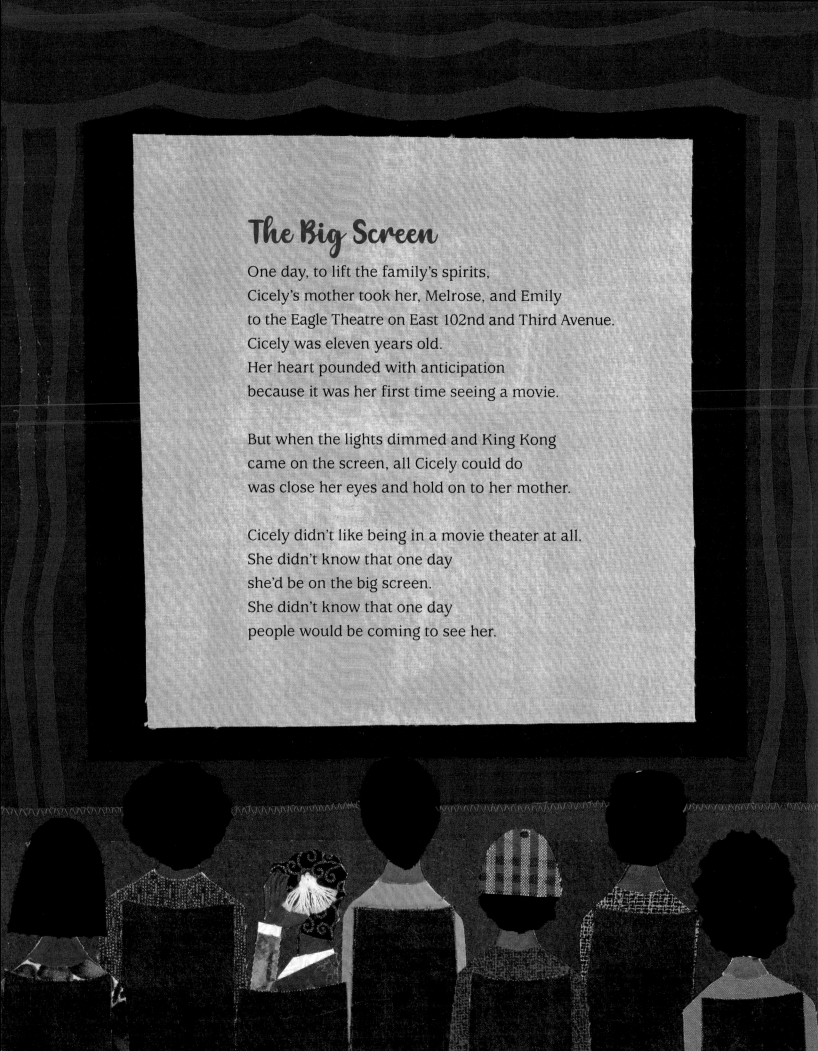

# The Big Screen

One day, to lift the family's spirits,
Cicely's mother took her, Melrose, and Emily
to the Eagle Theatre on East 102nd and Third Avenue.
Cicely was eleven years old.
Her heart pounded with anticipation
because it was her first time seeing a movie.

But when the lights dimmed and King Kong
came on the screen, all Cicely could do
was close her eyes and hold on to her mother.

Cicely didn't like being in a movie theater at all.
She didn't know that one day
she'd be on the big screen.
She didn't know that one day
people would be coming to see her.

# Piano Lessons

By twelve years old Cicely had finally
stopped sucking her thumb.
She was learning to play the piano
and needed her thumb on the keys,
not in her mouth.

She took lessons from Mrs. Wilson
for twenty-five cents per session.
She found a new comfort
in the magic of her hands.
They danced across the ramshackle upright piano
that sat in the living room.

By age fifteen she had taught herself
how to play the organ and played hymns
for the choir and congregation.

Her light burned brighter, brighter.
Especially when she played her favorite hymn.

*Just as I am, without one plea*
*But that Thy blood was shed for me*
*And that Thou bid'st me come to Thee*
*O Lamb of God, I come! I come.*

# True Style, True Beauty

At sixteen years old, Cicely was known
around the neighborhood
as the girl with talent and style.
No longer teased for being a twig of a girl
with buckteeth and dark skin.
She wore clothes
made by her mother's hands.
Pressed her hair with the hot comb
she inherited from her neighbor Miss Jones.
Folks loved her hair so much,
they asked Cicely if she'd do theirs.

Cicely made her rounds, pressing women's hair,
styling them to look their best.
On Sunday mornings her masterpieces were on display
throughout the congregation.
She made all these women feel and look beautiful:
updos, silky straight, parted in the middle, parted on the side,
buns, ponytails. Cicely's hands did it all.

She tried the hairstyles on herself too.
There was never a day of the week that
Cicely looked the same.

She worked on becoming even more beautiful
on the inside because she knew that who she was
on the inside mattered most.

# Purpose

Cicely's mother said,
*Maybe your purpose is to be a concert pianist*
*since you play so well.*
But Cicely knew that was not her calling.
She quit playing the piano because she didn't love it anymore.

*Maybe your purpose is to be a beautician,* her mother said.
*Since you're so good at pressing and styling.*
But Cicely knew that was not her calling.
She enjoyed doing hair, but it wasn't her passion.

Cicely's mother said, *Maybe your career will be as a secretary*
*since you can type a hundred words a minute.*
But Cicely knew that was not her calling.
Something on the inside told her,
*There's something else, there's more, there's more.*

# Destiny

While Cicely was window-shopping
at Lord & Taylor,
a man approached her and said,
*Excuse me, miss, are you a model?*
A confused Cicely replied, *I'm not a model.*
*Well, you should be,* the man said.

She took his advice and started taking classes
at Barbara Mae Watson's modeling agency in Harlem,
the first in the nation for Black models.
Cicely said yes to all kinds of jobs.
She modeled hats, shoes, purses, and even wigs.

It wasn't long before the twig of a girl
with buckteeth and dark skin
became one of the top Black models,
posing for spreads in *Jet, Ebony,* and *Vogue* magazines.

And still something on the inside told her,
*There's something else, there's more, there's more.*

**EBONY** 39¢

CICELY TYSON A STAR IS BORN

**JET** 15c

CICELY A STAR

**VOGUE**

CICELY TYSON FASHION QUEEN MOVIE STAR

# An Ordinary (Extraordinary) Day

Cicely dropped off a photograph at *Our World* magazine.
On her way out, she politely said hello to a woman waiting in the lobby.

After Cicely left the building, the woman asked,
*Who was that young lady who sashayed out of here?*

There was an independent movie being made
about a Black family, and Cicely was exactly
the type the director was looking for.

When Cicely first spoke to the director, she turned down the offer.
*I don't know anything about making a movie,* she said.

*Well,* the director said,
*I guess you'll find out.*

OUR WORLD

25¢

CICELY TYSON

# Leaving Home

Cicely agreed to read the script,
*The Spectrum*, to be polite.
She had no intention of being in the movie.
But as she read the words of the characters,
she got chills and couldn't stop reading.

The voice inside of her that had been telling her,
*There's something else, there's more,*
*there's more,*
told her to say yes.

The director was ecstatic to welcome
her to the cast,
but her mother was against it.
Because of her religious beliefs,
her mother didn't want
her daughter working in Hollywood.

*You can't stay here and do that,* she told Cicely.

So Cicely moved out.

# Shine On

Cicely missed seeing and talking with her mother.
But she was no longer the little girl
singing and playing the piano at church.
She was ready for bigger stages.

Cicely moved in with a friend and began taking
classes to become the best actress she could be.

During these years, she met actors
who the world would soon know
as legendary changemakers.
But Cicely knew them as friends.

Ruby Dee, Ossie Davis, Sidney Poitier,
Harry Belafonte, Isabel Sanford,

Diahann Carroll, Maya Angelou.
Cicely marveled at their brilliance, at their talent, at their grace.
Her light was bright, bright, bright right alongside theirs,

# Pride

Two years passed, and still Cicely had not seen her mother.
But that changed the night Cicely performed in the play *Dark of the Moon*
at the Harlem YMCA.

She invited her mother, and, to her surprise,
her mother came, with Emily at her side.

When Cicely stepped onto the stage,
butterflies fluttered in her belly.
Would her mother like the performance?
Would she make her mother proud?

Cicely knew exactly where her mother was sitting,
so she avoided looking at that side of the theater.
Under the dark lights and across the hushed audience,
she heard her mother call out,
*There she is! There's my String Bean.*

After the show, Cicely's mother came backstage,
beaming with pride. From that day forward,
she bragged about Cicely to anyone who would listen.
*My daughter, she's an actress.*
*I knew she'd be something big one day!*

The woman
with the thick curls,
so many, many years ago, who had said,
*Take care of that baby.*
*She's going to make you very proud one day . . .*
was right.

Black is too much bloodshed,
blood wasted.
Black is another
dream deferred.

Black is hair big like cumulus clouds,
flat and twisted, braided like knitted yarn,
morphed into sculptures.

Black is Motown records spinning
and spinning,
rejoicing and mourning,
mourning and rejoicing.

Black is loud and proud.
Black is boom box on shoulder,
turntables, and break dance battles.

Black is the tree planted by the water,
unmovable, unmovable.

Black is never forget:
we've come this far by faith.

# Natural & Proud

For the CBS drama *Between Yesterday and Today,*
Cicely decided to cut her hair and wear it natural
to better portray the character.

No Black actress had ever worn her hair natural
on television, and Cicely decided to change that.

She told the barber, *I want you to cut it as short as you can get it.*

*How's this?* the barber asked.

*Shorter.*

*How's this?* the barber asked.

*Shorter.*

*Are you sure?*

Cicely was sure. She was proud
of her hair and the many styles she could wear.

She wore her black hair like
a halo, like a crown.

# Strong, Black & Beautiful

Cicely vowed to only play roles that
showed the dignity and humanity of Black people.
She refused to portray negative Black characters,
even if it meant turning down money.
She only said yes to roles that sent chills up her spine.

She kept her promise and became known
for portraying strong Black women.

Rebecca in *Sounder*.
Binta, mother of Kunta Kinte in *Roots*.
Miss Jane Pittman in
*The Autobiography of Miss Jane Pittman*.
Harriet Tubman.
Coretta Scott King.

She brought the beauty and soul of Black women
to the screen and stage
and mesmerized audiences with her talent.

Cicely's acting was so outstanding
that she won three Emmy Awards,
one Screen Actors Guild Award, one Tony Award,
an honorary Oscar, and a Peabody Award.
She also won eight NAACP Image Awards.

With every role, she transformed herself,
drawing inspiration from the women of her childhood.
All those years of being quiet, of observing the world
and asking it questions, prepared her
for the women she portrayed.

She knew firsthand that Black women
were strong, beautiful.
And she brought that knowing
to every screen, every stage.

And still
there was more to come.

# Taking Action

Cicely used her voice to bring awareness
to social issues all around the world.

As a United Nations Goodwill Ambassador,
she traveled to Africa and visited hospitals and schools
in Ivory Coast, Burkina Faso, and Chad.
She donated money to provide stethoscopes,
blankets, linens, and pillows to local hospitals.
She offered support to women and children
suffering from famine.

Cicely believed she had to give
and be a blessing to others.

*We cannot do enough, we cannot give enough,* Cicely said.
*We have to give back.*

# 1990s–2010s

Black is fight the power
and *Yes We Can!*

Black is bended knee, is protest chant,
is *Come too far to give up now.*

# Showstopper

Button-covered minidresses,
chiffon capes, sculptural gowns,
animal prints, colorful head wraps
oversize furs, cashmere sweaters,
bell sleeves,
long trains, miniskirts,
ruffles and ruffles and ruffles,
vintage French silk,
diamonds, feathers, sequins,
earrings hanging like chandeliers.

Cicely made a statement
every time she entered a room.

She became a fashion icon,
known for wearing unique,
bold clothes
designed by her good friend,
the fashion designer
B Michael.

He dressed her in couture:
one-of-a-kind creations
for a one-of-a-kind soul.

# Supernova

Cicely played more than one hundred roles
in her lifetime.

Beyond the characters she played on stages and sets,
in real life she impacted many lives.
She received many awards and high recognition.

In 1995 a performing arts high school
in East Orange, New Jersey, was named after Cicely Tyson.
The school was just six houses away from where her father once lived.

Cicely didn't want the building to just have her name;
she wanted to be a presence at the school.
Some semesters she taught an acting class.
Sometimes she'd visit classrooms,
taking in students' art, listening to their stories.

In 2016 President Barack Obama awarded Cicely
the highest civilian honor, the Presidential Medal of Freedom.

*Cicely Tyson has not only exceeded as an actor,* he said.
*She has shaped the course of history.*

Even with all the awards, red carpets,
and stardom, what Cicely wanted most
was for people to know that she'd done her best.

# Cicely

Some called her friend; others called her teacher, mentor.
She was an award-winning actress, a fashionista,
a trendsetter, a gentle and wise woman.

She was a bright light
shining in a world that was sometimes dark,
sometimes unjust.

Nine decades she lived:
96 years. 35,105 days.

With each sunrise she was determined
to be better than the day before, to do good in the world,
to shine her light brighter and brighter.

And shine is exactly what she did.

## 2020s

Black is the ancestors' answered prayer.
Black is resilient, is the torch
passed on and on, generation to generation.

# Timeline

**1924** — Cicely Tyson is born on December 19 in New York City.

**1954** — Begins modeling career

**1956** — First film role in *Carib Gold*

**1961** — Stars in Jean Genet's off-Broadway play *The Blacks* with James Earl Jones. The play runs for more than 1,400 performances.

**1963–64** — Becomes the first African American to star in a TV drama with the release of *East Side/West Side*

**1972** — The movie *Sounder* is released. Cicely is nominated for a Golden Globe Award and an Academy Award.

**1974** — The TV film *The Autobiography of Miss Jane Pittman* is released. Cicely wins the Emmy Award for Best Actress.

**1977** — Inducted into the Black Filmmakers Hall of Fame

**1977** — The TV miniseries *Roots* is released. Cicely is nominated for a Primetime Emmy Award.

**1978** — The TV miniseries *King* is released. Cicely is nominated for a Primetime Emmy Award.

**1983** — Plays the lead in the Broadway show *The Corn Is Green*.

**2010** — The NAACP honors Cicely with the 95th Spingarn Medal.

**2013** — Wins the Tony Award for Best Actress for her role in the Broadway revival of *The Trip to Bountiful*

**2016** — Receives the Presidential Medal of Freedom from President Barack Obama

**2019** — Receives the Academy Honorary Award from the Academy of Motion Picture Arts and Sciences

**2020** — Inducted into the Television Fall of Fame

**2021** — January 28, Cicely Tyson passes peacefully in her Harlem home. Her funeral is held at the Abyssinian Baptist Church in Harlem on February 16.

# Thank You, Miss Tyson.

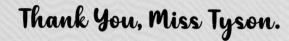

For Zora Neal Finnie-Myers and Sage Iyanu Green.
—R.W.

For Wadie, Frances, Nana, and Sarah,
the women who loved me,
and for my husband, Marcus—
I could not do this without you.
—S.S.

Amistad is an imprint of HarperCollins Publishers.

Cicely Tyson
Text copyright © 2024 by Renée Watson
Illustrations copyright © 2024 by Sherry Shine
Photo on page 48: *Promotional photo of American fashion model, film and TV
actress about 1970* by Pictorial Press Ltd / Alamy Stock Photo
All rights reserved. Manufactured in Italy.

Library of Congress Control Number: 2023948447
ISBN 978-0-06-321999-1

The artist used fabric, quilting, and embellishments to create the illustrations for this book.
Typography by Dana Fritts and Honee Jang
24 25 26 27 28   RTLO   10 9 8 7 6 5 4 3 2 1

First Edition